The Vacuum Effect

Christine Groethe

The Vacuum Effect: Harnessing the Universe's Energy for Success

Published by BooxAi

ISBN: 978-965-578-637-8

The Vacuum Effect

Harnessing the Universe's Energy for Success

Christine Groethe

Contents

Chapter 1

Introduction to the Vacuum Effect

The Power of the Universe

In the vast expanse of the universe, there lies an incredible source of energy just waiting to be harnessed. This power, which permeates every aspect of our existence, is often over-looked or ignored by many, but when understood and utilized, it has the potential to transform our lives in unimaginable ways.

Welcome to the subchapter titled "The Power of the Universe" from the book "The Vacuum Effect: Harnessing the Universe's Energy for Success."

The universe is a mindful entity, constantly in motion, responding to our thoughts and intentions. It operates under the principle that nature abhors a vacuum, meaning that empty spaces are naturally filled. This paradox is the key to unlocking the universe's power and manifesting our biggest life intentions.

To tap into the power of the universe, we must first become aware of our own thoughts and intentions. Our minds are like magnets, attracting the energy that resonates with our thoughts. By cultivating a positive and focused mindset, we align ourselves with the universe's energy, allowing it to flow through us.

THE SIX STEPS TO MANIFESTING OUR BIGGEST LIFE intentions are as follows:

1. Clarify your intention: Clearly define what you want to manifest in your life. Be specific and paint a vivid picture of your desired outcome.

2. Believe in the possibility: Have unwavering faith in the power of the universe and your ability to manifest your intentions. Trust that the universe will provide what you desire.

3. Align your thoughts and emotions: Cultivate positive thoughts and emotions that match your desired outcome. Visualize yourself already living your intention and feel the emotions associated with it.

4. Take inspired action: Act on the opportunities that present themselves. The universe will provide guidance and synchronicities that lead you closer to your intention. Trust your intuition and take inspired action.

5. Release attachment: Let go of any attachment to the

outcome. Trust that the universe knows what is best for you and will deliver it in the perfect timing.

6. Gratitude and surrender: Express gratitude for what you have already received and surrender to the universe's wisdom. Trust that everything is unfolding as it should.

By following these steps, you tap into the power of the universe and become a co-creator of your reality. The universe is abundant and ready to provide, but it requires your active participation. Embrace the paradox of the mindful universe, harness its energy, and watch as your biggest life intentions manifest before your eyes.

Understanding the Vacuum Effect

In the quest for success and fulfillment, we often come across the concept of the Vacuum Effect. This intriguing phenomenon has been described as the Universe's way of manifesting our deepest intentions and desires. By harnessing the energy of the Universe, we can unlock our true potential and create the life we've always dreamed of.

The Mindful Universe Paradox highlights the idea that the Universe hates a vacuum. It suggests that when we create space in our lives by letting go of negativity, limiting beliefs, and outdated patterns, we create a void that the Universe eagerly seeks to fill. This is where the Vacuum Effect comes into play – it is the process of attracting what we truly desire into our lives.

To harness the power of the Vacuum Effect, we need to

follow six essential steps. These steps serve as a roadmap to manifest our biggest life intentions and create a reality that aligns with our true purpose.

1. Clarify Your Intentions: The first step is to gain clarity on what we truly want. By defining our intentions with utmost precision, we send a clear signal to the Universe, enabling it to respond in kind.

2. Release Resistance: To create space for the Vacuum Effect to work its magic, we must let go of resistance and negative energy. This involves identifying and addressing any fears, doubts, or limiting beliefs that may be holding us back.

3. Cultivate Gratitude: Gratitude is a powerful force that amplifies the Vacuum Effect. By appreciating what we already have, we open ourselves up to receiving even more abundance and opportunities.

4. Visualize and Embody: Visualization is a tool that helps us create a mental blueprint of our desired reality. By vividly imagining ourselves living our intentions, we begin to align our thoughts, emotions, and actions with our desired outcomes.

5. Take Inspired Action: The Vacuum Effect requires us to take inspired action towards our intentions. It is not enough to simply visualize; we must also actively pursue our goals, seizing opportunities that come our way.

6. Trust and Surrender: Finally, we must trust in the process and surrender to the Universe's intelligence. Letting go of control and allowing the Vacuum Effect to unfold

naturally opens us up to unexpected miracles and synchronicities.

By understanding and applying the principles of the Vacuum Effect, we can tap into the limitless power of the Universe and manifest our biggest life intentions. Whether it's achieving career success, finding love and happiness, or cultivating personal growth, the Vacuum Effect has the potential to transform our lives in miraculous ways. Embrace this powerful concept, and let the Universe guide you towards your greatest desires.

The Importance of Harnessing Universal Energy

In today's fast-paced world, it is easy to get caught up in the chaos and lose sight of the bigger picture. We often find ourselves striving for success, chasing after material possessions, and neglecting our inner well-being. However, deep within the universe lies an incredible source of energy that can help us achieve our biggest life intentions and bring about true fulfillment. This subchapter will explore the importance of harnessing universal energy and how it can positively transform our lives.

The concept of the mindful universe paradox emphasizes that the universe hates a vacuum. Just as nature abhors an empty space, the universe seeks to fill our lives with energy, abundance, and purpose. When we tap into this universal energy, we align ourselves with the natural flow of life and open the doors to infinite possibilities.

Harnessing universal energy is not a complicated process. The book "The Vacuum Effect: Harnessing the Universe's Energy for Success" presents a practical six-step approach that anyone can follow to manifest their biggest life intention. These steps are designed to help us connect with the universal energy and channel it towards our desired outcomes.

The first step is to cultivate mindfulness and awareness. By quieting our minds and becoming present in the moment, we create space for the universe's energy to enter our lives. This allows us to tap into our intuition and gain clarity about our deepest desires.

The second step involves setting a clear intention. By clearly defining what we want to manifest, we create a powerful focus that guides the universal energy towards our goals. This step requires us to be specific and heartfelt in our intentions, as the universe responds to authenticity and passion.

The third step is to visualize our intentions as already achieved. By creating vivid mental images of our desired outcomes, we send a powerful signal to the universe that we are ready to receive what we desire. This step helps to strengthen our belief in the manifestation process and align our thoughts with the universal energy.

Taking inspired action is the fourth step in harnessing universal energy. It is not enough to simply visualize our intentions; we must also take consistent and purposeful action towards our goals. This step involves breaking down our intentions into manageable steps and staying committed to the journey.

The fifth step is to surrender and let go of attachment to the outcome. Trusting in the universe's infinite wisdom, we release any doubts or fears that may hinder the manifestation process. This step requires us to have faith in the timing and unfolding of events, knowing that the universe always works in our favor.

Finally, the sixth step involves expressing gratitude for what has already been received. By acknowledging the abundance in our lives, we create a positive vibration that attracts even more blessings. This step helps us maintain a state of gratitude and appreciation, further enhancing our connection to the universal energy.

Harnessing universal energy is not reserved for a select few; it is available to everyone. By understanding the importance of tapping into this energy and following the six steps outlined in "The Vacuum Effect: Harnessing the Universe's Energy for Success," we can manifest our biggest life intentions and experience true fulfillment. Embrace the mindful universe paradox, and let the universe's energy guide you towards a life of abundance and success.

How the Vacuum Effect Can Transform Your Life

In the vast expanse of the universe, there exists a powerful force known as the Vacuum Effect. This force, when harnessed, has the potential to transform every aspect of your life and bring about incredible success. Welcome to the subchapter titled "How the Vacuum Effect Can Transform Your Life" from the book "The Vacuum Effect: Harnessing the Universe's Energy for Success."

This subchapter aims to provide you with profound insights into the Vacuum Effect and how it can be utilized to manifest your biggest life intentions. Whether you are a skeptic or a believer, the principles discussed here are applicable to everyone and can be employed to create positive change in your life.

The Universe hates a vacuum, and this paradoxical concept lies at the core of the Vacuum Effect. It suggests that nature abhors emptiness and constantly seeks equilibrium. When you create a void in your life, whether it be in your thoughts, emotions, or physical space, the Universe rushes to fill it with something. This phenomenon can be harnessed to manifest your deepest desires and intentions.

To tap into the power of the Vacuum Effect, we present six transformative steps. These steps will guide you through the process of manifesting your biggest life intentions, helping you unlock your true potential and achieve remarkable success:

1. Embrace Mindfulness: Cultivate awareness of your thoughts, emotions, and actions. By staying present in the moment, you create space for the Universe to work its magic.

2. Set Clear Intentions: Clearly define what you desire and set specific, measurable, achievable, relevant, and time-bound (SMART) goals. The Universe responds to clarity and specificity.

3. Release Resistance: Let go of any doubts, fears, or limiting beliefs that may hinder your progress. Trust in the process and surrender to the Universe's infinite wisdom.

4. Take Inspired Action: Act upon the opportunities that come your way. The Universe rewards those who take decisive and inspired action towards their intentions.

5. Practice Gratitude: Express gratitude for what you already have while anticipating the manifestation of your desires. Gratitude amplifies the Vacuum Effect and attracts more abundance into your life.

6. Trust the Process: Have faith in the Universe's ability to bring your intentions to fruition. Trust that everything is unfolding perfectly, even if the path may seem uncertain at times.

By following these steps and harnessing the power of the Vacuum Effect, you can manifest your biggest life intentions and create a life filled with abundance, joy, and success. Embrace the paradox of the mindful universe and witness the transformative power it holds for everyone.

Chapter 2

The Mindful Universe Paradox

Exploring the Mind-Body Connection

The mind-body connection is a fascinating phenomenon that has been studied and explored for centuries. It is the understanding that our thoughts, emotions, and beliefs have a direct impact on our physical well-being. In recent years, this concept has gained significant attention as more and more people are realizing the power of harnessing this connection to improve their overall health and well-being.

In this subchapter, "Exploring the Mind-Body Connection," we delve into the profound implications of this connection and how it can be harnessed to manifest your biggest life intentions. We will explore the Mindful Universe Paradox and the concept that the universe hates a vacuum, providing you with six practical steps to manifest your deepest desires.

The Mindful Universe Paradox suggests that the universe is an intelligent, conscious entity that is responsive to our thoughts and intentions. By understanding and aligning ourselves with the laws of the universe, we can tap into its energy to manifest our biggest life intentions. This concept challenges us to become more mindful of our thoughts, beliefs, and emotions, as they shape the reality we experience.

To harness the power of the mind-body connection, we must first recognize the importance of self-awareness. This involves paying attention to our thoughts and emotions, identifying any negative patterns or limiting beliefs that may be holding us back. Through practices such as meditation, visualization, and positive affirmations, we can reprogram our minds and replace negative thoughts with positive ones.

The next step is to cultivate a deep sense of gratitude and trust in the universe. By expressing gratitude for what we already have and trusting that the universe is working in our favor, we create a positive, energetic vibration that attracts abundance and success into our lives.

Another crucial aspect of harnessing the mind-body connection is taking inspired action. It is not enough to simply visualize our intentions; we must also take concrete steps towards achieving them. This involves setting clear goals, creating a plan of action, and consistently working towards our dreams.

In this subchapter, we will guide you through a six-step process that combines these principles to help you manifest your biggest life intention. These steps include setting a clear intention, visualizing your desired outcome, aligning your thoughts and emotions, taking inspired action, cultivating gratitude, and surrendering to the universe's timing.

By exploring the mind-body connection and applying these principles, you have the power to transform your life and manifest your biggest dreams. Whether you seek financial abundance, vibrant health, loving relationships, or personal fulfillment, understanding and harnessing this connection can be the key to unlocking your true potential and living a life of purpose and joy.

Remember, the universe is always conspiring in your favor. Embrace the power of the mind-body connection and watch as your intentions become reality.

The Role of Consciousness in Manifestation

In the journey towards success and fulfillment, understanding the role of consciousness in manifestation is paramount. Consciousness, the state of being aware and perceiving one's surroundings, plays a vital role in shaping our reality and influencing the outcomes we desire. It is the driving force behind our thoughts, emotions, and actions, and when harnessed correctly, can propel us towards our biggest life intentions.

At its core, consciousness is the connection between the individual mind and the vast universe. It is through consciousness that we tap into the infinite energy and possibilities that surround us. The Universe, as a mindful entity, responds to our conscious thoughts and intentions, constantly interacting with us in a dynamic exchange of energy. This interaction forms the foundation of manifestation.

The Universe hates a vacuum, as it abhors emptiness and always seeks to fill it with energy. This principle is a fundamental aspect of manifestation. By consciously aligning our thoughts and intentions with what we wish to manifest, we create a powerful vacuum that draws the necessary energy and resources towards us. However, it is not enough to simply desire something; we must also believe in our ability to receive it. Our consciousness must be in harmony with our intentions for manifestation to occur.

To manifest our biggest life intentions, we can follow a six-step process rooted in the mindful universe paradox. Firstly, we must clearly define our intention, visualizing it with utmost clarity. This creates a powerful image in our minds, which serves as a guiding beacon for the Universe to align with. Secondly, we must cultivate unwavering belief and faith in our ability to manifest our intention. Doubt and skepticism only serve to block the flow of energy.

The third step involves releasing any resistance or negative emotions that may hinder our manifestation. This requires acknowledging and letting go of any limiting beliefs, fears, or doubts that may arise. By releasing these barriers, we create space for positive energy to flow freely.

The fourth step is to take inspired action towards our

intention. Manifestation is not about sitting back and waiting for things to happen; it involves actively participating in the process. By taking small and consistent steps towards our goal, we demonstrate our commitment and readiness to receive.

The fifth step involves practicing gratitude and appreciation for all that we already have. Gratitude is a powerful tool that amplifies positive energy and attracts more abundance into our lives. By focusing on what we are grateful for, we shift our consciousness towards abundance and create an energetic magnet for manifestation.

Finally, the sixth step is to surrender and trust in the process. Once we have set our intentions, aligned our consciousness, and taken inspired action, it is essential to let go and trust that the Universe will deliver. Surrendering control and allowing the natural flow of energy to unfold ensures that we are open to receiving the manifestation of our desires.

In conclusion, consciousness holds immense power in the manifestation process. By understanding and harnessing this power, we can tap into the Universe's energy and manifest our biggest life intentions. Through the mindful universe paradox and its six-step process, we can align our thoughts, beliefs, and actions to create a powerful vacuum that attracts the abundant energy required for manifestation. Remember, the Universe hates a vacuum, but it loves to fill it with the magic of manifestation.

Understanding the Paradox of the Mindful Universe

In this subchapter, we delve into the intriguing concept of the mindful universe and explore the paradox that it presents. The universe, as we know it, is a vast expanse of energy and matter, constantly in motion and evolving. It is a tapestry of interconnectedness and interdependence, where every action has a reaction, and every thought has a consequence. This profound understanding forms the basis of the mindful universe paradox.

The paradox arises from the idea that while the universe is abundant and full of possibilities, it also "hates a vacuum." This phrase, often attributed to Aristotle, implies that nature abhors emptiness and seeks to fill any void or vacuum. In the context of our lives, this paradox suggests that when we create a void or emptiness, the universe will naturally move to fill it.

Harnessing this paradox is a powerful tool for manifesting our biggest life intentions. By understanding that the universe seeks to fill voids, we can intentionally create space for our desires to come into existence. This requires us to engage in a six-step process that aligns our thoughts, actions, and intentions with the mindful universe.

Step 1: Awareness - Become aware of the thoughts, beliefs, and patterns that may be creating a void in your life. By acknowledging these areas of lack, you can begin to shift your focus towards abundance.

Step 2: Release - Let go of limiting beliefs and negative thought patterns that perpetuate the void. This step involves consciously choosing to release any resistance or attachment to outcomes.

Step 3: Intention - Clearly define your biggest life intention and align it with your values and purpose. This step involves setting a clear and specific goal that resonates deeply with you.

Step 4: Alignment - Align your thoughts, emotions, and actions with your intention. By consistently focusing on positive thoughts and emotions, you create a vibrational match for your desires.

Step 5: Trust - Trust in the process and have faith that the universe will fill the void with the resources, opportunities, and experiences necessary for your intention to manifest.

Step 6: Gratitude - Cultivate an attitude of gratitude for the abundance that already exists in your life. By expressing gratitude, you open yourself up to receiving even more blessings from the universe.

Understanding the paradox of the mindful universe empowers us to take control of our lives and consciously manifest our biggest intentions. By aligning our thoughts, actions, and intentions with the abundant nature of the universe, we become co-creators of our reality. Embrace the paradox, and watch as the universe fills the voids in your life with infinite possibilities and success.

Overcoming Limiting Beliefs and Embracing Possibility

In our journey towards success and fulfillment, one of the biggest obstacles we often face is our own limiting beliefs. These beliefs, deeply ingrained in our subconscious minds, hold us back from reaching our full potential and embracing the endless possibilities that the universe has to offer. However, by recognizing and overcoming these limiting beliefs, we can harness the energy of the universe and manifest our biggest life intentions.

The first step in overcoming limiting beliefs is self-awareness. Take a moment to reflect on your thoughts and beliefs about yourself and your abilities. Are there any recurring thoughts that hold you back? Do you find yourself doubting your capabilities or fearing failure? By identifying these limiting beliefs, you can begin to challenge and change them.

Once you have identified your limiting beliefs, the next step is to question their validity. Often, these beliefs are based on past experiences or the opinions of others. Ask yourself, "Is this belief based on facts or is it just a perception?" By questioning the validity of your limiting beliefs, you can start to see them for what they truly are - mere illusions that have no power over you.

To truly overcome limiting beliefs, it is essential to replace them with empowering ones. Affirmations and positive self-talk can play a significant role in this process.

Repeat empowering statements such as "I am capable of achieving greatness" or "I am deserving of success" to reprogram your subconscious mind.

Another powerful technique to overcome limiting beliefs is visualization. Take some time each day to visualize yourself living your desired life, achieving your goals, and embracing the abundance of the universe. By consistently visualizing your desired outcomes, you align your energy with the universe and attract the opportunities needed to manifest your intentions.

Lastly, surround yourself with supportive and like-minded individuals. Seek out communities or mentors who believe in the power of the universe and share your vision for success. By surrounding yourself with positivity and encouragement, you create a fertile ground for personal growth and manifestation.

Remember, the universe is abundant, and it wants to support you in realizing your dreams. By overcoming limiting beliefs and embracing the infinite possibilities, you can harness the energy of the universe and manifest your biggest life intentions. Trust in yourself and the universe, and watch as the magic unfolds.

Chapter 3

The Universe Hates a Vacuum

Unveiling the Nature of the Universe

In this subchapter, "Unveiling the Nature of the Universe," we embark on a fascinating journey to explore the underlying principles that govern the universe we live in. From ancient philosophical debates to modern scientific discoveries, we delve into the mysteries that have captivated humanity for centuries.

The nature of the universe has always been a source of wonder and awe. People from all walks of life, regardless of age, background, or beliefs, have contemplated its origins, purpose, and the intricate web of interconnectedness that binds everything together. This subchapter aims to shed light on these profound questions and provide you with a glimpse into the extraordinary nature of our reality.

We begin by examining the Mindful Universe Paradox,

a concept that highlights the paradoxical relationship between consciousness and the physical world. As we delve into this topic, we explore how our thoughts, intentions, and perceptions can shape our reality and influence the course of our lives. By understanding the power of our minds and the interconnectedness of all things, we unlock the potential to manifest our biggest life intentions.

Furthermore, we explore the age-old adage, "The Universe hates a vacuum." This intriguing phrase takes on a metaphorical meaning in our exploration, suggesting that the universe abhors emptiness and seeks to fill it with energy and intention. We unveil the secrets behind this statement and discover how we can harness the universe's energy to manifest our desires and create a life filled with abundance and success.

To assist you on this transformative journey, we present you with six practical steps to manifest your biggest life intention. These steps, grounded in ancient wisdom and modern scientific understanding, provide a roadmap for unlocking your true potential and aligning yourself with the abundant energy of the universe. By following these steps with dedication and mindfulness, you will learn to harness the power of intention and consciously create the life you desire.

Whether you are a seeker of knowledge, a spiritual explorer, or simply curious about the nature of the universe, this subchapter is for you. Its contents are designed to be accessible to everyone, regardless of their background or level of understanding. So, join us as we embark on a captivating journey of self-discovery, unveiling the nature of the universe and discovering the keys to manifesting your biggest life intention.

The Law of Attraction and the Vacuum Effect

In the grand tapestry of the universe, there exists a powerful force that governs our lives - the Law of Attraction. This fundamental principle suggests that we attract into our lives whatever we focus on, whether positive or negative. It is a concept that has intrigued and fascinated individuals across cultures and generations, offering a glimpse into the extraordinary potential that lies within each of us.

But what if I told you that there is another force at play, working in tandem with the Law of Attraction? This force is known as the Vacuum Effect, and it holds the key to harnessing the universe's energy for unparalleled success.

The Vacuum Effect is based on the age-old adage that the universe abhors a vacuum. Just as nature abhors emptiness and seeks to fill it, so too does the universe seek to fill the voids in our lives. This principle is deeply intertwined with the Law of Attraction, as it complements and amplifies its effects.

To harness the power of the Vacuum Effect, we must first identify our biggest life intention. What is it that we truly desire? Whether it is financial abundance, fulfilling relationships, or personal growth, the Vacuum Effect teaches us that we must create a void in our lives for these desires to manifest.

The six steps to manifesting your biggest life intention through the Vacuum Effect are simple yet profound. First, you must clarify your intention with unwavering clarity. Define the outcome you seek and visualize it with absolute certainty.

Second, you must release any resistance or doubt that may hinder the manifestation process. Trust in the universe's ability to deliver and let go of any negative beliefs or limiting thoughts.

Next, take inspired action towards your intention. The Vacuum Effect requires us to actively participate in the manifestation process. This may involve setting goals, creating a plan, or taking small steps towards our desired outcome.

The fourth step is to create space in your life for your intention to materialize. This may involve decluttering your physical space, releasing toxic relationships, or letting go of old beliefs that no longer serve you. By creating a void, you open up the space for the universe to fill it with your desires.

Fifth, cultivate an attitude of gratitude. Express gratitude for the blessings that already exist in your life, as well as the ones that are yet to come. Gratitude is a powerful magnet that attracts more of what we appreciate.

Finally, surrender to the process. Trust that the universe

knows the perfect timing for your desires to manifest. Let go of control and embrace the flow of life.

By understanding and harnessing the power of the Vacuum Effect in conjunction with the Law of Attraction, we can create a life of limitless possibilities. Remember, the universe is ready and willing to support us in our journey towards success and fulfillment. It is up to us to harness its energy and manifest our biggest life intention.

The Effects of Resistance and Lack in Your Life

In our journey towards success and fulfillment, we often encounter resistance and lack. These two elements can have profound effects on our lives, shaping our experiences and holding us back from manifesting our biggest life intentions. Understanding these effects is crucial for everyone, especially those who resonate with the niche of the "Mindful Universe Paradox: The Universe hates a vacuum: Six steps to manifest your biggest life intention."

Resistance is a force that opposes our desires and goals. It can manifest in various forms, such as self-doubt, fear, or external obstacles. When we resist, we create friction between our intentions and the natural flow of the universe. This friction hinders our progress and prevents us from tapping into the unlimited energy available to us. In essence, resistance keeps us stuck in a cycle of dissatisfaction and unfulfilled potential.

Lack, on the other hand, refers to a sense of scarcity or deprivation. When we focus on what we lack, whether it be money, love, or opportunities, we reinforce a mindset of scarcity. This mindset constricts our ability to receive abundance from the universe. It becomes a self-fulfilling prophecy, attracting more lack into our lives and perpetuating a cycle of limitation.

The effects of resistance and lack are intertwined. When we resist, we often focus on what we lack, fueling a negative feedback loop. This combination creates a vacuum in our lives, depleting us of the energy needed to manifest our biggest intentions. It is as if the universe responds to our resistance and lack by withholding the very things we desire.

To break free from this cycle, we must cultivate awareness and shift our mindset. By acknowledging our resistance and recognizing the areas of lack in our lives, we can begin to release these limiting beliefs. Embracing a mindset of abundance and gratitude opens up the channels for the universe's energy to flow freely. We can then align ourselves with our intentions and work towards manifesting them.

The path to success and fulfillment requires us to transcend resistance and lack. By understanding the effects they have on our lives, we can consciously choose to let go of these limitations. Through the six steps outlined in the "Mindful Universe Paradox," we can harness the energy of the universe and manifest our biggest life intentions. It is through this process that we can truly thrive and create a life of purpose, abundance, and joy.

Breaking Free from Scarcity Mindset

In the journey towards success and fulfillment, one of the biggest obstacles we often face is the scarcity mindset. This mindset, deeply ingrained in our society, constantly reminds us of limitations and lack. It is the belief that there is never enough to go around, that opportunities are scarce, and that abundance is only for a select few. However, in order to harness the universe's energy for success, it is crucial to break free from this scarcity mindset and embrace a mindset of abundance.

The universe is a vast and abundant source of energy, constantly flowing and expanding. It is not limited by scarcity or lack, but rather it thrives on abundance and infinite possibilities. By shifting our mindset from scarcity to abundance, we align ourselves with the natural flow of the universe and open ourselves up to limitless opportunities.

To break free from the scarcity mindset, it is important to first recognize and challenge our limiting beliefs. Often, these beliefs are deeply rooted in our subconscious mind, formed by past experiences and societal conditioning. By becoming aware of these beliefs and questioning their validity, we can start to dismantle them and replace them with empowering beliefs.

The next step is to practice gratitude and cultivate a mindset of abundance. Gratitude is a powerful tool that shifts our focus from what we lack to what we already have. By acknowledging and appreciating the abundance that exists in our lives, we attract more abundance into our reality. This can be done through simple practices like keeping a gratitude journal or regularly expressing gratitude for the blessings in our lives.

Another important aspect of breaking free from a scarcity mindset is embracing a mindset of possibility and expansion. Instead of seeing limitations and lack, start focusing on the infinite possibilities and potential that exist within and around you. By adopting a growth mindset, you open yourself up to new opportunities, learning experiences, and personal growth.

Lastly, surround yourself with a supportive and positive community. The people we surround ourselves with greatly influence our mindset and beliefs. Surrounding yourself with individuals who share a mindset of abundance and growth will help reinforce and amplify your own positive mindset.

By breaking free from the scarcity mindset and embracing a mindset of abundance, you tap into the unlimited potential of the universe. You become a magnet for success, opportunities, and fulfillment. Remember, the universe hates a vacuum, and it is ready to fill your life with abundance once you release the scarcity mindset and harness its energy for your biggest life intentions.

Chapter 4

The Six Steps to Manifest Your Biggest Life Intention

Step 1: Clarifying Your Life Intention

In this first step, we will delve into the importance of clarifying your life intention and how it can help you harness the universe's energy for success. Understanding and defining your life intention is crucial as it sets the foundation for manifesting your biggest dreams and desires.

Our lives can sometimes feel like a vacuum, devoid of purpose and meaning. However, the universe abhors a vacuum, and when we clarify our life intention, we create a powerful gravitational force that attracts the energy needed to manifest our goals.

The first question you must ask yourself is: What is your true life intention? Take a moment to reflect on this question, for it holds the key to unlocking your greatest potential. Your life intention is not simply a goal or a wish; it is a deep-rooted desire that aligns with your core values and brings you fulfillment.

To clarify your life intention, it is essential to engage in self-reflection and introspection. Consider your passions, talents, and what truly brings you joy. What do you want to contribute to the world? What legacy do you want to leave behind? These are the guiding questions that will help you uncover your life intention.

Once you have identified your life intention, write it down and make it tangible. This could be in the form of a statement, a vision board, or any other medium that resonates with you. By externalizing your intention, you are sending a clear message to the universe, affirming your commitment to manifesting your desires.

Remember, clarifying your life intention is an ongoing process. As you grow and evolve, you may find that your intention shifts or expands. Embrace this journey of self-discovery and allow yourself the freedom to refine your intention as needed.

By taking the time to clarify your life intention, you are setting the stage for the universe to work its magic. Each step you take towards aligning your actions with your intention brings you closer to manifesting your dreams. Stay tuned for Step 2, where we will explore the power of visualization and how it can further amplify your manifestation process.

In conclusion, clarifying your life intention is the first step on your journey towards harnessing the universe's energy for success. It is an essential process that allows you to align your actions with your deepest desires. By defining your life intention and making it tangible, you create a powerful force that attracts the energy needed to manifest your biggest dreams. Stay tuned for the next steps in the Mindful Universe Paradox: The Universe hates a vacuum: Six steps to manifest your biggest life intention.

Step 2: Setting Powerful Intentions

In the journey to manifesting your biggest life intention, setting powerful intentions is a crucial step that cannot be overlooked. Your intentions are like the guiding compass that directs the universe's energy towards creating the reality you desire. By setting powerful intentions, you align your thoughts, emotions, and actions with the universe's infinite potential, enabling you to manifest your dreams and aspirations with greater ease and efficiency.

The process of setting powerful intentions begins with clarity. Take some time to reflect on what you truly desire in life. What is your biggest life intention? Is it to achieve financial abundance, find a fulfilling career, or cultivate deep and meaningful relationships? Whatever it may be, allow yourself to dream big and envision it in vivid detail.

Once you have a clear picture of your intention, it's time to infuse it with power. Power lies in the emotions and beliefs you attach to your intention. Emotionally connect with the outcome you desire by feeling the joy, excitement, and gratitude as if it has already manifested in your life.

Believe with unwavering faith that the universe is conspiring in your favor and that your intention is already on its way to you.

To further enhance the power of your intentions, consider creating a visualization or vision board. Visualization is a powerful tool that allows you to mentally rehearse your desired outcome, activating the creative forces of the universe. Visualize yourself living your intention, experiencing all the emotions, sights, and sounds associated with it. Allow yourself to fully immerse in this experience and feel the positive energy flowing through you.

Alongside visualization, affirmations can be another effective tool for setting powerful intentions. Craft positive and empowering affirmations that reflect your intention as if it has already been achieved. Repeat these affirmations daily, preferably in the morning and evening, to reprogram your subconscious mind and align your thoughts with your desired outcome.

Remember, setting powerful intentions is not a one-time event but an ongoing process. Continuously reinforce your intentions through daily rituals, such as meditation and journaling. These practices help you stay focused, maintain a positive mindset, and strengthen your connection with the universe.

By setting powerful intentions, you become an active participant in the co-creation of your reality. You harness the universe's energy and align it with your desires, allowing the manifestation process to unfold effortlessly. So, dive deep into your intentions, infuse them with power, and watch as the universe conspires to bring your biggest life intention to fruition.

In the next step, we will explore the importance of taking inspired action towards your intentions and how it propels you further along the path of manifestation. Stay tuned for Step 3: Taking Inspired Action.

Step 3: Aligning Your Thoughts and Emotions

In this subchapter, we will delve into the crucial step of aligning your thoughts and emotions to harness the universe's energy for success. As we continue our journey towards manifesting our biggest life intention, it is imperative to recognize the power of our thoughts and emotions in shaping our reality.

The mindful universe paradox teaches us that the universe hates a vacuum – it abhors emptiness. Therefore, if we want to manifest our desires, we must fill our minds and hearts with positive thoughts and emotions that align with our intentions. This alignment creates a powerful vibrational frequency that attracts the opportunities and resources necessary for our success.

To begin aligning our thoughts and emotions, we must first cultivate mindfulness – the practice of being fully present in the moment. By cultivating mindfulness, we become aware of our thoughts and emotions, allowing us to consciously choose which ones we want to amplify and manifest. Mindfulness also helps us detach from negative thoughts and emotions that may hinder our progress.

Once we have cultivated mindfulness, we can begin consciously directing our thoughts towards our desired outcome. Visualization exercises are an effective way to align our thoughts with our intentions. Close your eyes and imagine yourself already living your biggest life intention. Feel the excitement, joy, and gratitude that comes with achieving it. By consistently visualizing this reality, you send a clear message to the universe about what you want to manifest.

Alongside aligning our thoughts, we must also align our emotions. Emotions are powerful energy in motion, and they have the ability to either attract or repel what we desire. Therefore, it is essential to cultivate positive emotions such as love, joy, gratitude, and confidence. By consciously choosing to feel these emotions, we create a vibrational frequency that resonates with abundance, thereby attracting more of it into our lives.

To further align our thoughts and emotions, we can incorporate daily affirmations and gratitude practices into our routine. Affirmations are positive statements that affirm our desires as already being true. By repeating these affirmations daily, we reprogram our subconscious mind to believe in our ability to manifest our intentions. Gratitude, on the other hand, shifts our focus from lack to abundance, allowing us to appreciate what we already have while attracting more of it.

As we continue to align our thoughts and emotions, remember that consistency and patience are key. Rome wasn't built in a day, and neither will your biggest life intention manifest overnight. Trust in the process, believe in your power, and keep aligning your thoughts and emotions with your desired outcome. The universe, in all its infinite wisdom, will conspire to manifest your intentions when the time is right.

Step 4: Taking Inspired Action

In this subchapter, we will explore the crucial step of taking inspired action towards manifesting your biggest life intention. As we delve deeper into the Mindful Universe Paradox, we discover that the Universe despises a vacuum and yearns for us to actively participate in its grand design. By aligning our actions with our intentions, we can harness the Universe's energy to propel us towards success.

Taking inspired action involves more than just mindlessly going through the motions. It requires a conscious connection to our inner desires and a willingness to step out of our comfort zones. When we align our actions with our intentions, we create a powerful synergy that can move mountains and attract the opportunities and resources we need to achieve our goals.

To take inspired action, we must first clarify our intentions. What is it that we truly desire? What steps can we take to bring our dreams into reality? By setting clear intentions and visualizing our desired outcomes, we create a roadmap for our actions.

Once our intentions are clear, it's time to overcome any limiting beliefs or fears that may be holding us back. Often, we sabotage our own progress by doubting our abilities or fearing failure. By acknowledging and releasing these self-imposed limitations, we create space for new possibilities to emerge.

Taking inspired action also involves staying present and attuned to the signs and synchronicities that the Universe sends our way. These signs can be subtle or obvious, but they all serve as guideposts along our journey. By staying open and receptive to these messages, we can make course corrections when needed and seize opportunities that align with our intentions.

It's important to remember that taking inspired action is not about forcing or striving. It's about surrendering to the flow of the Universe and allowing it to guide us towards our goals. When we trust in the process and take action from a place of inspired alignment, we tap into the infinite power of the Universe and become co-creators of our own destinies.

So, let go of any resistance or hesitation, and embrace the magic of inspired action. Trust that the Universe will support you every step of the way as you take bold strides towards manifesting your biggest life intention. Remember, the Universe hates a vacuum, and by actively participating in its grand design, you can unlock the limitless potential that lies within you.

Step 5: Trusting the Process and Letting Go

Trusting the process and letting go are two fundamental aspects of harnessing the universe's energy for success. In this chapter, we will explore how these steps can help you manifest your biggest life intention and create a mindful universe paradox.

Trusting the process requires a leap of faith. It means believing that the universe has a plan for you and that everything is unfolding perfectly, even if it may not seem that way at first. Often, we find ourselves resisting the natural flow of life, trying to control every outcome and micromanage every situation. However, this only leads to frustration and disappointment.

To trust the process, you must surrender to the idea that you are co-creating with the universe. This means releasing the need for control and allowing things to unfold naturally. It involves developing a deep sense of faith in yourself and the universe, knowing that you are on the right path and that everything is happening for your highest good.

Letting go is the next step in this transformative journey. It involves releasing attachments, expectations, and limiting beliefs that no longer serve you. When you hold onto things tightly, whether it's a specific outcome or a past hurt, you create resistance and block the flow of energy. By letting go, you open yourself up to new possibilities and allow the universe to work its magic.

Letting go doesn't mean giving up or being passive. It means detaching yourself from the outcome and embracing the present moment. It means surrendering to the natural rhythm of life and trusting that everything will unfold in divine timing.

Trusting the process and letting go go hand in hand. When you trust, you let go of control, and when you let go, you trust in the process. Together, they create a powerful synergy that aligns you with the universe's energy and propels you towards your biggest life intention.

Remember, the universe hates a vacuum. When you release what no longer serves you, you create space for new opportunities and experiences to flow into your life. Trusting the process and letting go are essential ingredients for manifesting your desires and living a fulfilled life.

In the next chapter, we will explore step 6, which focuses on taking inspired action and aligning your thoughts, feelings, and actions with your intentions. Get ready to embrace the power of manifestation and unlock the limitless possibilities that await you.

Step 6: Embracing Gratitude and Appreciation

Gratitude and appreciation are two powerful emotions that can transform our lives and help us manifest our biggest life intentions. In this step, we will explore how embracing gratitude and appreciation can harness the energy of the universe and propel us towards success.

Gratitude is the practice of acknowledging and being thankful for the blessings and abundance in our lives. It is about recognizing the positive aspects, big or small, and expressing our appreciation for them. When we cultivate gratitude, we shift our focus from what is lacking to what we already have, opening ourselves up to receive more.

Appreciation, on the other hand, goes beyond gratitude. It is about recognizing the value and worth of something or someone. When we appreciate, we acknowledge the efforts, qualities, and contributions that make a positive impact on our lives. By expressing our appreciation, we not only uplift others but also create a positive ripple effect in the universe.

The mindful universe paradox teaches us that the universe hates a vacuum. When we fill our hearts and minds with gratitude and appreciation, we create a space for more blessings and abundance to flow into our lives. This step empowers us to tap into the universal energy and align ourselves with the forces that support our intentions.

Practicing gratitude and appreciation is simple yet profound. Start by keeping a gratitude journal, where you write down three things you are grateful for every day. It could be as simple as a beautiful sunset, a kind gesture from a stranger, or the love and support of our loved ones. By consistently focusing on the positive aspects of our lives, we begin to shift our mindset and attract more positivity.

In addition to journaling, make it a habit to express appreciation to those around you. Take a moment to acknowledge and thank someone for their contribution, whether it is a friend, family member, colleague, or even yourself. By acknowledging the value in others, we create an environment of positivity and attract more opportunities for growth and success.

Remember, embracing gratitude and appreciation is a continuous practice. As we cultivate these emotions, we become more attuned to the abundant possibilities that surround us. By harnessing the energy of the universe through gratitude and appreciation, we can manifest our biggest life intentions and live a life of purpose and fulfillment.

So, let us embark on this journey of gratitude and appreciation, knowing that by doing so, we are aligning ourselves with the limitless power of the universe. Embrace the abundance that awaits and watch your intentions unfold gracefully and easily. The universe is ready to conspire in your favor, and it all begins with gratitude and appreciation.

Chapter 5

Practical tools and Techniques for Harnessing Universal Energy

Visualization and Affirmations

In the journey towards success and fulfillment, one powerful tool that is often overlooked is the practice of visualization and affirmations. These two practices can be transformative, helping us tap into the immense power of the universe and manifest our biggest life intentions.

Visualization is the art of creating vivid mental images of our desired outcomes. By harnessing the power of our imagination, we can create a detailed picture of what we want to achieve or experience in our lives. When we visualize, we activate the creative forces within us and send a clear message to the universe about our intentions. This practice is not limited to our goals or desires; it can also be used to cultivate a positive mindset, improve relationships, or enhance overall well-being.

To effectively visualize, find a quiet and comfortable space where you can fully immerse yourself in the process. Close your eyes and take a few deep breaths to center yourself. Then, start to create a mental image of your desired outcome. See the details, feel the emotions, and engage all your senses as if you are already living your intention. The more vivid and real you make the visualization, the stronger the signal you send to the universe.

Affirmations are positive statements that we repeat to ourselves regularly. They help to reprogram our subconscious mind and align our thoughts and beliefs with our intentions. Affirmations are a powerful way to counter negative self-talk and limiting beliefs that may be holding us back from achieving our goals. By consciously choosing empowering affirmations and repeating them daily, we can shift our mindset and attract positive experiences into our lives.

When crafting affirmations, use present tense and keep them positive, specific, and realistic. For example, instead of saying, "I will be successful," say, "I am successful in all areas of my life." Repeat your affirmations with conviction and conviction, believing that they are already true. This sends a clear message to the universe that you are ready to receive what you desire.

The practice of visualization and affirmations is a powerful combination that can help us tap into the universe's energy and manifest our biggest life intentions. By consistently engaging in these practices, we align our thoughts, feelings, and beliefs with our desires, creating a powerful magnet for success. So, take a few moments each day to visualize your dreams and affirm your intentions. Watch as the universe responds to your focused energy and brings your desires to life. Remember, you have the power to create the life you desire.

In this subchapter, we delve into the fascinating realm of meditation and mindfulness practices and their profound impact on harnessing the universe's energy for success. These practices are not exclusive to any particular group; rather, they are accessible and beneficial to everyone, regardless of age, background, or beliefs. Whether you are a beginner or an experienced practitioner, this chapter will provide valuable insights to help you manifest your biggest life intention.

Meditation and Mindfulness Practices

At its core, meditation is a powerful tool that allows us to connect with our inner selves and tap into the abundant energy of the universe. By quieting our minds and focusing our attention, we can cultivate a state of mindfulness that opens doors to infinite possibilities. Mindfulness, on the other hand, is the art of being fully present in the current moment, embracing it with non-judgmental awareness.

The practice of meditation and mindfulness invites us to shift our perspective and become aware of the interconnectedness of all things. We create a space within ourselves to let go of negative thoughts, worries, and distractions, and instead, embrace the limitless potential that surrounds us. Through this practice, we align our intentions with the universe, allowing the energy to flow freely and manifest our deepest desires.

In this subchapter, we explore six steps to manifest your biggest life intention using the mindful universe paradox. We start by setting a clear intention, planting the seed of desire in our minds. Next, we cultivate a sense of gratitude and appreciation for what we already have, recognizing that abundance is ever-present in our lives.

We then move on to the practice of visualization, using our imagination to vividly picture our desired outcomes. This step helps to strengthen our belief in the manifestation process and allows us to tap into the creative power of our minds. Following visualization, we engage in affirmations and positive self-talk, reprogramming our subconscious minds to align with our intentions.

The fifth step involves taking inspired action, actively working towards our goals while remaining open to the signs and synchronicities that the universe presents along the way. Finally, we surrender and trust in the process, releasing attachment to the outcome and allowing the universe to work its magic.

By incorporating these meditation and mindfulness practices into your daily routine, you will discover a profound sense of peace, clarity, and purpose. The universe responds to your intentions when you create the space to listen and align yourself with its energy. Embrace the mindful universe paradox, and watch as your biggest life intention manifests before your eyes.

Journaling and Self-Reflection

In the fast-paced world we live in, it is easy to become overwhelmed and lose touch with ourselves. The demands of work, family, and society often leave us feeling disconnected and lost. However, there is a powerful tool that can help us navigate these challenges and rediscover our true selves – journaling and self-reflection.

Journaling is the act of putting pen to paper and allowing your thoughts and emotions to flow freely. It is a private space where you can express yourself without judgment or limitations. By writing down your experiences, dreams, and fears, you create a tangible record of your journey through life.

Self-reflection, on the other hand, is the process of introspection and examination of one's thoughts, actions, and beliefs. It involves taking a step back from the chaos of everyday life and delving deep into your core values and desires. Self-reflection allows you to gain clarity and insight into who you truly are and what you want to achieve.

The combination of journaling and self-reflection is a powerful practice that can help you harness the universe's energy for success. By taking the time to reflect on your experiences and emotions, you become more self-aware and better equipped to make conscious choices that align with your deepest desires.

When you journal, you create a space for self-expression and self-discovery. As you write, you may uncover hidden fears or limiting beliefs that have been holding you back. By acknowledging these obstacles, you can begin to release them and make room for new possibilities.

Moreover, journaling and self-reflection allow you to set intentions and manifest your biggest life goals. By writing down your intentions and regularly reflecting on your progress, you become more focused and committed to achieving them. The act of journaling itself can be a form of visualization, helping you to visualize your dreams and make them a reality.

To harness the full potential of journaling and self-reflection, it is essential to follow these six steps:

1. Set aside dedicated time for journaling and self-reflection.

2. Create a sacred space where you can write freely and without distractions.

3. Be honest and authentic in your journaling, allowing your true thoughts and emotions to surface.

4. Regularly review and reflect on your journal entries to track your progress and identify areas for growth.

5. Use positive affirmations and visualization techniques to reinforce your intentions.

6. Practice gratitude and celebrate your successes along the way.

Remember, journaling and self-reflection are not just for writers or those on a spiritual journey. They are tools that can benefit anyone seeking self-discovery, personal growth, and success. By harnessing the power of the universe through journaling and self-reflection, you can unlock your fullest potential and manifest your biggest life intentions. Start today and witness the transformative power of this simple yet profound practice.

In this subchapter, we delve into the powerful realm of energy clearing and balancing techniques, unlocking the secrets to harness the Universe's energy for success. Whether you are a skeptic or a believer, these techniques are designed for everyone, regardless of their background or beliefs. By understanding and applying the principles of energy clearing and balancing, you can tap into the limitless potential of the mindful universe paradox and manifest your biggest life intention.

Energy Clearing and Balancing Techniques

Energy clearing is the process of removing any stagnant or negative energy that may be obstructing your path to success. Just like a cluttered room prevents free movement, energy blockages hinder the flow of abundance and achievement in our lives. Through various practices such as meditation, visualization, and breathwork, you can release these blockages and create space for positive energy to flow.

Balancing energy is equally crucial, as it ensures that our

physical, mental, and emotional well-being are in harmony. Balancing techniques help align our energy centers, known as chakras, allowing us to function optimally in all aspects of life. These techniques involve practices like yoga, tai chi, and Reiki, which promote a balanced energy flow and restore equilibrium to our being.

One of the most effective energy-clearing techniques is visualization. By visualizing a bright light cleansing your body and surroundings, you can actively remove negative energy and replace it with positive vibrations. Another powerful technique is sound therapy, which utilizes various frequencies and vibrations to release stagnant energy and promote healing.

To balance your energy, mindfulness plays a crucial role. By being present in the moment, you can better understand the subtle shifts in your energy and take action accordingly. Mindful breathing exercises, such as deep belly breathing, can help restore balance and bring you back to the present.

Understanding the Universe's dislike for a vacuum is also key to manifesting your biggest life intention. By creating space within yourself and your surroundings, you invite the Universe to fill it with abundance and success. Energy clearing and balancing techniques provide the necessary tools to create that space and maintain a harmonious flow of energy.

In conclusion, energy clearing and balancing techniques are accessible to everyone, regardless of their background or beliefs. By practicing these techniques, you can tap into the mindful universe paradox and manifest your biggest life intention. Embrace these tools, unlock the power within, and witness their transformative effects on your journey towards success and fulfillment.

Chapter 6

Applying the Vacuum Effect to Different Areas of Life

Manifesting Abundance and Financial Success

In this subchapter, we delve into the intriguing concept of manifesting abundance and financial success. The Universe is a vast and mysterious entity, and it constantly seeks to maintain balance and harmony. Understanding how to harness its energy can provide us with the tools to manifest our biggest life intentions and achieve true abundance.

The Mindful Universe Paradox: The Universe hates a vacuum, introduces us to the principle that the Universe abhors emptiness and seeks to fill any void with energy. By leveraging this principle, we can learn how to attract abundance and financial success into our lives.

STEP 1: CLARIFY YOUR INTENTIONS

To manifest abundance, it is crucial to have a clear understanding of what we truly desire. Take the time to reflect on your goals and aspirations, and write them down. This clarity will serve as a guiding light in your journey towards financial success.

STEP 2: ALIGN YOUR THOUGHTS AND EMOTIONS

Thoughts and emotions are powerful forces that shape our reality. Align your thoughts with the intention of abundance and success. Embrace positive emotions such as gratitude, joy, and excitement, as they attract positive energy and opportunities.

STEP 3: VISUALIZE YOUR DESIRED OUTCOME

Create a vivid mental image of what your financial success looks like. Imagine yourself living in abundance, experiencing financial freedom, and enjoying the fruits of your labor. Visualization enhances the manifestation process by sending a clear message to the Universe.

STEP 4: TAKE INSPIRED ACTION

While manifestation involves tapping into the Universe's energy, it is essential to take practical steps towards your goals. Act upon your desires, seize opportunities, and be open to new possibilities. The Universe will respond to your proactive nature and guide you towards abundance.

STEP 5: RELEASE RESISTANCE AND TRUST THE PROCESS

Let go of any doubts, fears, or limiting beliefs that may hinder your progress. Trust in the Universe's ability to provide and have faith in your own capabilities. By relinquishing resistance, you create space for abundance to flow into your life.

STEP 6: EXPRESS GRATITUDE

Expressing gratitude is a powerful practice that amplifies the manifestation process. Acknowledge and appreciate the abundance that already exists in your life. Gratitude creates a positive energy field that attracts more abundance and financial success.

BY FOLLOWING THESE SIX STEPS, YOU CAN TAP INTO THE energy of the Universe and manifest abundance and financial success. Remember, this process is not about instant gratification but about aligning yourself with the flow of abundance. With dedication, persistence, and belief in yourself, you can create a life of prosperity and fulfillment. Start harnessing the Universe's energy today and unlock the door to your biggest life intentions.

Cultivating Healthy Relationships and Love

In the grand tapestry of life, relationships hold a profound significance. They shape our experiences, emotions, and overall well-being. Whether it's the bond between friends, family, or romantic partners, healthy relationships are the pillars that provide support, love, and growth. In this subchapter, we delve into the secrets of cultivating healthy relationships and love, drawing upon the principles of the mindful universe paradox and the vacuum effect.

Love, the most powerful force in the universe, is not something that happens by chance. It is a conscious choice and a continuous effort. To manifest healthy relationships and love, we must first understand that the universe abhors a vacuum. Just as a vacuum seeks to be filled, so too do our relationships require constant nurturing and attention. We cannot expect love to flourish without putting in the necessary work.

The first step in cultivating healthy relationships is self-awareness. By understanding our own needs, desires, and limitations, we can better navigate the complexities of relationships. Self-reflection allows us to identify any negative patterns or unresolved issues that may hinder our ability to love and be loved. Only by healing ourselves can we create a fertile ground for love to thrive.

Communication is another vital aspect of healthy relationships. Open and honest communication is the bridge that connects hearts and minds. It is through effective communication that we can express our feelings, needs, and concerns, while also listening empathetically to our loved ones. By fostering a safe and non-judgmental space for communication, we can build trust and deepen our connections.

Forgiveness is a transformative practice that can mend even the most broken relationships. Holding onto grudges and resentment creates an energetic blockage, preventing love from flowing freely. By embracing forgiveness, we release ourselves from the burden of the past and create space for healing and growth. It is important to remember that forgiveness is not an act of condoning, but rather a choice to let go and move forward.

Lastly, cultivating healthy relationships requires conscious effort and commitment. Just as a garden needs constant care, love needs to be nurtured daily. This entails showing appreciation, offering support, and making quality time for our loved ones. By prioritizing our relationships and making them a foundation of our lives, we create a harmonious balance that resonates with the universe's energy.

In conclusion, cultivating healthy relationships and love is a lifelong journey. By understanding the principles of the mindful universe paradox and the vacuum effect, we can manifest our deepest intentions for love and connection.

Through self-awareness, communication, forgiveness,

and commitment, we can create a nurturing and thriving environment for our relationships to flourish. Remember, love is not something to be found, but rather something to be cultivated. So, let us embark on this beautiful journey of love together.

Enhancing Career and Professional Growth

In today's fast-paced and competitive world, enhancing career and professional growth has become a top priority for individuals across all walks of life.

Whether you are a recent graduate, a mid-career professional, or even someone considering a career change, the need to continuously evolve and grow in your chosen field is vital to achieve success and fulfillment. This subchapter will explore various strategies and techniques to help you harness the universe's energy and manifest your biggest career intentions.

One of the fundamental principles in achieving career growth is adopting a mindful approach. The Mindful Universe Paradox teaches us that by being present and aware of our thoughts, actions, and surroundings, we can tap into the abundance of opportunities that the universe has to offer. Being mindful enables us to identify our strengths, weaknesses, and areas for improvement, allowing us to make better decisions and take proactive steps towards career advancement.

To manifest your biggest career intentions, it is crucial to set clear and specific goals. By defining what you want to achieve and creating a roadmap to get there, you create a powerful intention that aligns your energy with your desired outcome. Visualize yourself already achieving your goals and take inspired actions that bring you closer to your vision.

Another key aspect of career growth is continuous learning and self-improvement. Embrace a growth mindset that encourages you to constantly expand your knowledge and acquire new skills. Seek out opportunities for professional development, such as attending workshops conferences, or pursuing advanced certifications. Additionally, consider finding a mentor or joining professional networks to gain valuable insights from experienced individuals in your industry.

Networking and building strong relationships are also essential in enhancing your career. Connect with like-minded professionals, both within and outside your organization, to exchange ideas, collaborate on projects, and uncover potential career opportunities. Cultivating a strong professional network can open doors to new possibilities and help you stay ahead in your field.

Lastly, never underestimate the power of perseverance and resilience. The journey towards career growth is often accompanied by challenges and setbacks. However, by cultivating a positive mindset and learning from failures, you can bounce back stronger and use these experiences to propel yourself towards greater success.

Remember, the universe hates a vacuum, and by

actively engaging in your career growth and taking intentional steps towards your goals, you create space for new opportunities to manifest. Embrace the paradox and harness the universe's energy to enhance your career and professional growth. Your biggest intentions are within reach, and by aligning your actions with the principles discussed in this subchapter, you can achieve the success and fulfillment you desire.

Improving Health and Well-being

In today's fast-paced and stressful world, it is crucial to prioritize our health and well-being. The mind and body are interconnected, and when one suffers, the other is affected as well. In this subchapter, we will explore practical ways to improve our health and well-being, drawing inspiration from the mindful universe paradox and the concept that the universe hates a vacuum. By harnessing the universe's energy and following six steps, we can manifest our biggest life intentions and create a life filled with health and vitality.

The first step towards improving health and well-being is to cultivate a mindful and positive mindset. By practicing mindfulness, we become aware of our thoughts, emotions, and physical sensations. This self-awareness allows us to identify and release negative patterns that may be hindering our well-being. Embracing positivity and gratitude helps us shift our focus towards the present moment and appreciate the beauty of life.

The second step involves nourishing our bodies with nutritious foods and adopting a holistic approach to wellness. Eating a balanced diet rich in fruits, vegetables, whole grains, and lean proteins provides our bodies with the necessary nutrients to thrive. Additionally, incorporating regular exercise, sufficient sleep, and stress management techniques such as meditation or yoga contribute to overall well-being.

The third step is to create a supportive environment. Surrounding ourselves with positive and like-minded individuals can significantly impact our mental and emotional state. Engaging in healthy relationships, seeking support when needed, and avoiding toxic influences are essential for our well-being.

The fourth step is to practice self-care regularly. Taking time for oneself is not selfish but rather a necessity for personal growth and well-being. Engaging in activities that bring joy, relaxation, and rejuvenation, such as hobbies, reading, or taking walks in nature, allows us to recharge and replenish our energy.

The fifth step is to embrace balance in all areas of life. Striving for a work-life balance, setting boundaries, and prioritizing self-care are vital for maintaining good health and preventing burnout. By finding equilibrium in our daily routines, we create space for growth, happiness, and fulfillment.

The final step is to align our actions and intentions with

our deepest desires and life purpose. Understanding our values and aligning our actions with them brings a sense of meaning and fulfillment. By living in alignment with our true selves, we tap into the universe's energy and manifest our biggest life intentions.

Improving health and well-being is a lifelong journey that requires commitment, self-reflection, and mindful actions. By implementing these six steps, we can harness the universe's energy and create a life filled with vibrant health, happiness, and success. Remember, the universe hates a vacuum – by prioritizing our well-being, we allow for the manifestation of our biggest life intentions. Start today and embrace a life of vitality and fulfillment!

Expanding Personal and Spiritual Development

In today's fast-paced and often chaotic world, it is easy to get caught up in the daily grind and neglect our personal and spiritual growth. However, nurturing our inner selves is essential for living a fulfilled and purposeful life. In this subchapter, "Expanding Personal and Spiritual Development," we will explore the importance of self-discovery and provide six practical steps to manifest your biggest life intention.

Our personal and spiritual development is an ongoing journey that requires attention and commitment. It is about gaining a deeper understanding of ourselves, our purpose, and our connection to the world around us. By expanding our personal and spiritual development, we open doors to new opportunities, enhance our well-being, and ultimately manifest our biggest life intention.

The first step towards expanding personal and spiritual development is self-reflection. Take the time to understand your values, beliefs, and desires. Ask yourself what truly brings you joy and fulfillment. This introspection will serve as a foundation for your growth.

Next, embrace mindfulness. Mindfulness allows us to be fully present in each moment, cultivating a deeper awareness of ourselves and our surroundings. Through mindfulness, we can develop a greater appreciation for life and tap into our inner wisdom.

Another crucial aspect of personal and spiritual development is setting intentions. By clearly defining what we want to manifest in our lives, we align our thoughts and actions with our desired outcomes. This step involves visualizing our goals and affirming them with positive statements.

To support our expansion, it is essential to cultivate a daily practice. This could include meditation, journaling, or engaging in activities that bring us joy and peace. Consistency in our practice will deepen our connection with ourselves and the universe.

Furthermore, seeking knowledge and learning from others is vital. Surrounding ourselves with like-minded individuals and mentors who inspire us can accelerate our growth. Reading books, attending workshops, and engaging in meaningful conversations will expand our perspectives and provide valuable insights.

Lastly, taking inspired action is fundamental in manifesting our biggest life intention. As we expand our personal and spiritual development, we must be proactive in pursuing our goals. It is through action that we turn our dreams into reality.

In conclusion, expanding personal and spiritual development is a transformative journey that empowers us to live our best lives. By incorporating self-reflection, mindfulness, intention setting, daily practice, seeking knowledge, and taking inspired action, we can manifest our biggest life intention. Embrace this path of growth, and watch as your life unfolds in ways you never thought possible. Remember, the universe hates a vacuum, so fill it with your intentions and let the universe conspire to bring you success and abundance.

Chapter 7

Overcoming Challenges and Obstacles in Manifestation

Identifying and Addressing Blocks and Resistance

In our journey towards success and fulfillment, it is essential to recognize and overcome the blocks and resistance that may hinder our progress. These barriers can manifest in various forms, such as limiting beliefs, self-doubt, fear of failure, or even external obstacles. In this subchapter, we will explore effective strategies to identify and address these blocks, allowing us to harness the universe's energy for our greatest intentions.

The first step in overcoming blocks and resistance is self-awareness. We must take the time to reflect on our thoughts, emotions, and behaviors to identify any patterns or beliefs that may be holding us back. Through mindfulness and introspection, we can uncover the underlying causes of our resistance and gain clarity about our true desires and intentions.

Once we have identified these blocks, it is crucial to address them head-on. One powerful technique is reframing our limiting beliefs. By challenging and replacing negative thoughts with positive affirmations, we can shift our mindset and open ourselves to new possibilities. Additionally, seeking support from mentors, coaches, or like-minded individuals can provide valuable insights and guidance to help us navigate through these challenges.

Fear often plays a significant role in blocking our progress. To overcome fear, we must cultivate courage and take calculated risks. Embracing failure as a learning opportunity rather than a setback allows us to grow and move forward. It is important to remember that the universe supports us in our endeavors, and by facing our fears, we align ourselves with its abundant energy.

External obstacles can also impede our progress. It is essential to recognize that these challenges are part of our journey and not insurmountable roadblocks. By adopting a proactive mindset and seeking creative solutions, we can find alternative paths to success. Moreover, cultivating patience and persistence enables us to navigate around or overcome these obstacles as we continue to manifest our greatest intentions.

In conclusion, identifying and addressing blocks and resistance is a crucial step towards harnessing the universe's energy for success. By cultivating self-awareness, reframing limiting beliefs, facing our fears, and overcoming external obstacles, we can unlock our true potential and manifest our biggest life intentions. Remember, the universe hates a vacuum, and by removing these blocks, we create space for abundance and fulfillment to flow into our lives. Embrace the process, trust in the universe, and watch as your dreams become your reality.

Dealing with Doubt and Impatience

In our journey towards success and manifesting our biggest life intentions, doubt and impatience often become stumbling blocks that hinder our progress. These negative emotions can drain our energy and prevent us from fully harnessing the universe's energy. However, by understanding and effectively dealing with doubt and impatience, we can overcome these challenges and continue on the path to success.

Doubt is a natural human response when faced with uncertainty or unfamiliar territory. It creeps into our minds, whispering thoughts of failure and questioning our abilities. But we must remember that doubt is merely a perception and not an absolute truth. It is essential to recognize doubt for what it is - a temporary feeling that can be overcome.

To deal with doubt, we must first acknowledge it. Accepting that doubt is a part of the journey allows us to confront it head-on. Instead of allowing doubt to paralyze us, we can use it as a catalyst for growth. By questioning our doubts and examining the underlying beliefs that fuel them, we can challenge and replace them with empowering thoughts. Surrounding ourselves with positive influences and seeking support from like-minded individuals can also help dispel doubt and keep us motivated.

Impatience, on the other hand, stems from our desire for immediate results. In our fast-paced society, we often expect instant gratification and become frustrated when things don't unfold as quickly as we would like. However, it's important to remember that the universe operates on its own timeline, and everything happens in divine timing.

To overcome impatience, we must cultivate patience and trust in the process. This involves practicing mindfulness and staying present in the moment. Rather than focusing solely on the end goal, we can appreciate the small steps and progress we make along the way. By shifting our perspective and viewing delays or setbacks as opportunities for growth and learning, we can maintain a positive mindset and keep moving forward.

In conclusion, dealing with doubt and impatience is crucial for harnessing the universe's energy for success. By acknowledging doubt and challenging it with empowering thoughts, we can overcome its grip on us. Similarly, cultivating patience and trust in the process helps us combat impatience and stay aligned with the universe's timeline. Remember, the journey towards success is not always smooth, but by addressing doubt and impatience, we can manifest our biggest life intentions and harness the power of the mindful universe paradox.

Handling Setbacks and Failure

In the journey towards success, setbacks and failure are inevitable companions. They are not signs of weakness or incompetence but rather crucial stepping stones on the path to achieving greatness. In this subchapter, we will delve into the art of handling setbacks and failure, understanding that they are not roadblocks but opportunities for growth and learning.

1. Embrace the Mindful Universe Paradox:

The Universe hates a vacuum, and this paradoxical truth holds immense power when it comes to handling setbacks and failure. Instead of resisting or avoiding these experiences, embrace them wholeheartedly. Recognize that setbacks are temporary and failure is not a reflection of your worth. By accepting this paradox, you enable yourself to view setbacks as valuable lessons that propel you forward.

2. Shift Your Perspective:

When faced with setbacks and failure, it is crucial to adopt a growth mindset. See these experiences as opportunities for personal development and self- improvement. Instead of dwelling on the negative aspects, ask yourself, "What can I learn from this?" By shifting your perspective, setbacks transform into catalysts for growth and pave the way for future success.

3. Practice Resilience:

Resilience is a powerful tool in handling setbacks and failure. Understand that setbacks are a natural part of any journey and resilience is key to bouncing back. Cultivate a resilient mindset by focusing on your strengths, maintaining a positive outlook, and surrounding yourself with supportive individuals. Remember, it is not about avoiding failure, but rather about bouncing back stronger each time.

4. Learn from Mistakes:

Failure is not the end; it is an opportunity to learn and improve. Analyze your mistakes, identify areas for growth, and make necessary adjustments. By learning from your failures, you gain valuable insights that guide you towards future success. Embrace failure as a teacher, and let it fuel your determination to excel.

5. Seek Support:

Handling setbacks and failure can be challenging, but you don't have to face them alone. Reach out to mentors, friends, or support groups who can provide guidance and encouragement. Sharing your experiences and seeking advice from others who have overcome similar obstacles can provide valuable insights and help you navigate through difficult times.

6. Stay Committed to Your Intention:

Remember your biggest life intention and stay committed to it. Setbacks and failure are temporary detours on your path to success. The key is to remain focused and determined, even when faced with adversity. Forge ahead with an unwavering belief in your abilities and the knowledge that setbacks are merely stepping stones towards your ultimate goal.

In conclusion, setbacks and failure are not to be feared but embraced as integral parts of the journey towards success. By adopting a growth mindset, practicing resilience, learning from mistakes, seeking support, and staying committed to your intention, you will harness the power of the universe and manifest your biggest life intention. Embrace the vacuum effect and let setbacks propel you towards greatness.

Staying Persistent and Focused on Your Intention

In the journey towards success, staying persistent and focused on your intention is crucial. It is essential to understand that the universe operates in mysterious ways, and by harnessing its energy, you can manifest your biggest life intention. In this subchapter, we will explore the significance of persistence and focus and provide six practical steps to help you achieve your goals.

Persistence is the key to overcoming obstacles and challenges that may arise on your path to success. It is about having the determination and resilience to keep going, even when things get tough. The universe rewards those who persist in their endeavors, as it recognizes the unwavering commitment and unwavering belief in one's intention.

To stay persistent, it is crucial to remain focused on your intention. Distractions may tempt you to deviate from your path, but by staying focused, you can align your thoughts, actions, and energy towards your goal. This focused mindset allows you to tap into the universe's energy and channel it towards manifesting your intention.

HERE ARE SIX PRACTICAL STEPS TO HELP YOU STAY persistent and focused on your intention:

1. Clarify Your Intention: Clearly define what you want to manifest in your life. Be specific and visualize the outcome you desire.

2. Create a Vision Board: Compile images, quotes, and symbols that represent your intention and place them on a vision board. This visual representation will serve as a constant reminder of your goal.

3. Set Daily Intentions: Start each day by setting small, achievable intentions that align with your larger goal. This practice will help you stay focused and motivated.

4. Practice Mindfulness: Cultivate a mindful approach to life, staying present in the moment and aware of your thoughts and actions. Mindfulness will prevent you from being derailed by negative thoughts or distractions.

5. Surround Yourself with Supportive People: Surround yourself with individuals who believe in your intention and offer encouragement. Their positive energy will help you stay persistent and focused.

6. Celebrate Milestones: Acknowledge and celebrate your progress along the way. Recognizing your achievements will boost your motivation and reinforce your belief in your intention.

Remember, the universe hates a vacuum, and by staying persistent and focused, you can harness its energy to manifest your biggest life intention. Stay committed, believe in yourself, and trust in the process. Success is within your reach.

Chapter 8

Amplifying Your Results with Gratitude and Service

The Power of Gratitude in Manifestation

In this subchapter, we will explore the incredible power of gratitude in the process of manifestation. Gratitude is a force that can transform our lives and help us align with the universe's energy to bring about our biggest life intentions. Whether you are familiar with the concept of manifestation or new to it, understanding the role of gratitude can be a game-changer in your journey towards success.

Gratitude is more than just saying "thank you" for the things we have. It is a state of mind, a way of being that opens up channels for abundance and positive energy to flow into our lives. When we express gratitude, we are acknowledging the blessings and abundance that already exist, and in doing so, we attract more of it. The universe responds to our feelings and vibrations, and when we are grateful, we emit a frequency that resonates with the energy of manifestation.

To harness the power of gratitude in manifestation, we need to cultivate a daily gratitude practice. This can be as simple as starting each day by listing three things you are grateful for. By focusing on what you appreciate, you shift your mindset towards abundance and create a positive momentum that carries throughout your day. Additionally, expressing gratitude for future manifestations as if they have already occurred helps to bring them into reality.

Gratitude also plays a crucial role in the process of letting go and surrendering to the universe. When we are attached to our desires and outcomes, we create resistance and block the flow of manifestation. However, by practicing gratitude, we release this attachment and trust that the universe will bring us what is truly meant for us. Gratitude allows us to surrender and have faith in the process, knowing that everything is unfolding in divine timing.

Furthermore, gratitude has the power to shift our perspective and bring us into a state of alignment with our intentions. When we focus on what we appreciate, we raise our vibration and attract more positive experiences. As we align with the energy of gratitude, we become a magnet for manifestation, effortlessly attracting our biggest life intentions.

In conclusion, gratitude is a powerful tool in the process of manifestation. By cultivating a daily gratitude practice, letting go of attachment, and shifting our perspective, we can harness the universe's energy for success. Whether you are familiar with manifestation or new to it, incorporating gratitude into your journey will help you align with the mindful universe paradox and manifest your biggest life intentions. Embrace the power of gratitude and unlock the limitless possibilities that await you.

Giving Back and Helping Others

Subchapter: Giving Back and Helping Others

In this subchapter, we delve into the powerful concept of giving back and helping others, exploring how it aligns with the universe's energy and contributes to our personal success. Whether you are seeking fulfillment, abundance, or simply a greater sense of purpose, incorporating acts of kindness and generosity into your life can have a profound impact.

THE UNIVERSE OPERATES ON THE PRINCIPLE OF abundance, constantly flowing and expanding. When we embody this mindset, we tap into the inherent power of giving and create a vacuum effect that attracts positive energy and opportunities. By embracing the philosophy of "helping others helps yourself," we unlock a wellspring of possibilities.

Giving back can take various forms, and it is not limited to monetary contributions or grand gestures. Acts of kindness, compassion, and empathy have the ability to transform lives, both for the recipient and the giver. It could be as simple as lending a listening ear to a friend in need or volunteering at a local charity. The key is to cultivate a mindset of selflessness and look for opportunities to make a difference, no matter how small.

When we give without expecting anything in return, we shift our focus from scarcity to abundance. This shift in perspective opens doors to new connections, opportunities, and synchronicities that can propel us towards our biggest life intentions. The act of giving becomes a catalyst for manifestation, as we align ourselves with the positive energy of the universe.

Moreover, helping others provides us with a sense of purpose and fulfillment. It reminds us of our interconnectedness and the power of collective action. By contributing to the well-being of others, we create a ripple effect that spreads positivity and inspires others to do the same. In essence, the act of giving back becomes a vehicle for personal growth and transformation.

In this subchapter, we will explore practical ways to incorporate giving back into our lives. We will discuss the importance of cultivating a mindset of abundance, the benefits of selfless acts, and the various avenues through which we can make a positive impact. By embracing the vacuum effect through giving, we set ourselves on a path towards success, fulfillment, and a deeper connection with the universe.

Remember, the universe thrives on the energy of giving, and as we contribute to the betterment of others, we create a vacuum that attracts abundance into our own lives. So, let us embark on this journey of giving back and helping others, knowing that by doing so, we are harnessing the universe's energy for our ultimate success.

Creating a Positive Ripple Effect in the Universe

In this subchapter, we delve into the powerful concept of creating a positive ripple effect in the universe. As human beings, we are all connected, and our actions, thoughts, and intentions have the potential to impact not only our own lives but also the world around us. This idea forms the basis of the Mindful Universe Paradox: The Universe hates a vacuum - Six steps to manifest your biggest life intention.

The universe is constantly in motion, and it abhors a vacuum. Just as nature abhors empty spaces and seeks to fill them, so too does the universe seek to fill the voids created by negative energy and actions. This creates an opportunity for us to harness the universe's energy and channel it towards manifesting our biggest life intentions.

The first step in creating a positive ripple effect is to become mindful of our thoughts and actions. By cultivating awareness and being present in each moment, we can begin to observe the impact we have on ourselves and those around us. This self-awareness allows us to make conscious choices that align with our values and intentions.

Next, we must tap into our inner power and set clear intentions. By identifying our biggest life intention and visualizing it with vivid detail, we can send a powerful message to the universe. This intention acts as a guiding force, shaping our thoughts, actions, and interactions with others.

However, it is not enough to simply have intentions; we must also take action. The third step involves actively working towards our goals and dreams. Each small step we take creates a ripple effect that spreads positivity and inspiration to those around us. By leading by example, we inspire others to follow suit and create their own positive ripples.

The fourth step is to embrace gratitude and appreciation. Expressing gratitude for the blessings and opportunities in our lives opens us up to receive even more abundance from the universe. This gratitude creates a ripple effect of positivity, attracting more positive experiences and people into our lives.

Additionally, we must cultivate compassion and kindness towards others. The fifth step involves recognizing the interconnectedness of all beings and treating others with respect and empathy. By extending a helping hand, offering a kind word, or simply listening without judgment, we create a positive ripple that can have far-reaching effects.

Finally, we must believe in the power of our intentions and have faith in the universe. The sixth step involves trusting that our positive actions will make a difference and manifest our biggest life intention. This unwavering belief strengthens our resolve and keeps us focused on creating a positive ripple effect.

By following these steps and embracing the Mindful Universe Paradox, we have the potential to create a positive ripple effect that not only transforms our own lives but also influences the world around us. Together, let us harness the universe's energy for success and manifest our biggest life intentions, while spreading love, compassion, and positivity to everyone we encounter.

Maintaining the Vacuum Effect for Long-Term Success

Chapter 9

*Maintaining the Vacuum Effect for
Long Term Success*

Integrating the Vacuum Effect into Your Daily Life

In our fast-paced and chaotic world, finding inner peace and achieving success can often feel daunting. However, by harnessing the power of the vacuum effect, you can tap into the boundless energy of the universe and manifest your biggest life intentions. This subchapter will guide you through six simple steps to integrate the vacuum effect into your daily life, helping you unlock your true potential and achieve the success you desire.

Step 1: Cultivate Mindfulness

The first step towards integrating the vacuum effect is to cultivate mindfulness. By being fully present in each moment, you become aware of the opportunities and possibilities that surround you. Practice meditation, deep breathing exercises, or engage in activities that calm your mind and allow you to connect with your inner self.

Step 2: Define Your Life's Intention

To harness the power of the vacuum effect, it is essential to have a clear understanding of your life's intention. Take some time to reflect on your deepest desires and aspirations. Write them down and visualize them as if they have already been achieved. This clarity will help the universe align its energy with your intentions.

Step 3: Release Resistance

Often, resistance and negative beliefs can hinder our ability to manifest our intentions. Let go of any doubts, fears, or limiting beliefs that may be holding you back. Embrace positivity and affirmations to reprogram your subconscious mind and align it with the universe's energy.

Step 4: Take Inspired Action

The vacuum effect works in conjunction with action. While the universe aligns its energy with your intentions, taking inspired action towards your goals is vital. Break your intentions into small, achievable steps and consistently work towards them. Trust the process and remain open to unforeseen opportunities that may arise.

Step 5: Express Gratitude

Expressing gratitude is a powerful way to amplify the vacuum effect. Each day, take a moment to acknowledge and appreciate the blessings in your life. Gratitude creates a positive energy flow, attracting more abundance and success.

Step 6: Surrender and Trust

Lastly, surrender to the process and trust that the universe works in your favor. Let go of the need to control every aspect of your life and have faith that everything is unfolding as it should. Trust that the vacuum effect will bring you closer to your desired outcomes.

INTEGRATING THE VACUUM EFFECT INTO YOUR DAILY life invites the universe's energy to support and guide you towards manifesting your biggest life intention.

Embrace mindfulness, define your intentions, release resistance, take inspired action, express gratitude, and surrender to the process. You have the power to create the life you desire – let the vacuum effect be your guide.

Practicing Self-Care and Self-Compassion

In the fast-paced and demanding world we live in, it's easy to get caught up in the pursuit of success and forget about taking care of ourselves. However, self-care and self-compassion are not only essential for our overall well-being but also crucial for manifesting our biggest life intentions. In this subchapter, we will explore the importance of self-care and self-compassion and provide six practical steps to help you harness the universe's energy for success.

Self-care is about deliberately and consciously taking care of your physical, emotional, and mental health. It involves recognizing your needs and making choices that prioritize your well-being. When we neglect self-care, we become drained, stressed, and unable to perform at our best. By engaging in self-care practices such as exercise, proper nutrition, and sufficient rest, we replenish our energy levels and create a solid foundation for success.

Self-compassion, on the other hand, is about treating ourselves with kindness, understanding, and acceptance. Often, we are our harshest critics, setting impossibly high standards and beating ourselves up when we fall short. By cultivating self-compassion, we free ourselves from the burden of perfectionism and create a nurturing environment for growth and achievement.

To PRACTICE SELF-CARE AND SELF-COMPASSION effectively, we suggest the following six steps:

1. Reflect: Take time to reflect on your current self-care practices and identify areas that need improvement. Ask yourself what activities bring you joy and make you feel rejuvenated.

2. Prioritize: Make self-care a non-negotiable part of your daily routine. Schedule time for activities that nourish your mind, body, and soul.

3. Set boundaries: Learn to say no to commitments that do not align with your well-being. Setting boundaries protects your energy and allows you to focus on what truly matters.

4. Practice self-compassion: Treat yourself with kindness and understanding, just as you would a close friend. Challenge negative self-talk and replace it with positive affirmations.

5. Practice mindfulness: Engage in mindfulness activities such as meditation, deep breathing, or journaling. These practices help you stay present and reduce stress.

6. Seek support: Surround yourself with individuals who support your self-care journey. Share your goals and struggles with loved ones who can provide encouragement and accountability.

By practicing self-care and self-compassion, you create a harmonious relationship with yourself and the universe. Remember, the universe hates a vacuum, but it also rewards those who prioritize their well-being. When you take care of yourself, you become a magnet for success, manifesting your biggest life intentions effortlessly.

Whether you are embarking on a spiritual journey or seeking personal growth, integrating self-care and self-compassion into your life will lead you on a path of fulfillment, abundance, and success. Start today, and watch as the universe aligns to support your greatest intentions.

Evolving and Expanding Your Intentions

In this subchapter, we delve into the transformative process of evolving and expanding your intentions, as outlined in the book " The Vacuum Effect: Harnessing the Universe's Energy for Success." Whether you are a skeptic or a believer, this chapter will provide valuable insights and practical steps to help you manifest your biggest life intention.

The concept of the Mindful Universe Paradox states that the universe abhors a vacuum, meaning that it is constantly seeking to fill empty spaces with energy and potential. By understanding and harnessing this paradox, we can actively shape our reality and manifest our deepest desires.

The first step in evolving your intentions is self-reflection. Take a moment to truly understand what you want to manifest in your life. Dig deep and uncover your true passions, dreams, and goals. Once you have a clear vision, it's time to expand your intention beyond its current boundaries. Allow yourself to dream bigger, to think beyond what you initially believed possible. By expanding your intention, you open up a wealth of new possibilities and opportunities.

Next, it's crucial to align your intentions with your beliefs and values. Your intentions must be in harmony with your core being for them to manifest successfully. If there is a misalignment, take the time to reassess and adjust your intentions accordingly. This step ensures that you are working towards goals that truly resonate with your authentic self.

Once you have a clear and expanded intention, it's time to take action. The universe responds to deliberate and consistent action. Break down your intention into smaller, manageable steps and create a plan of action. Each step you take brings you closer to your desired outcome, and the universe will respond accordingly.

Throughout this process, it is important to remain open and flexible. The universe may present opportunities and synchronicities that are different from what you originally envisioned. Embrace these moments and trust that they are leading you towards your ultimate intention.

Lastly, practice gratitude and celebrate every milestone along the way. Gratitude is a powerful tool that amplifies positive energy and attracts more abundance into your life. By acknowledging and appreciating the progress you have made, you create a positive mindset that further fuels your manifestation process.

In conclusion, evolving and expanding your intentions is a vital step in manifesting your biggest life intention. By engaging in self-reflection, expanding your vision, aligning with your values, taking deliberate action, remaining open, and practicing gratitude, you can tap into the universe's energy and manifest the life you desire. Remember, the universe hates a vacuum, and it is eagerly waiting to fill your intentions with its abundant energy.

Chapter 10

Embracing a Life of Abundance and Fulfillment

Celebrating Your Manifestations and Successes

Subchapter: Celebrating Your Manifestations and Successes

In this subchapter, we delve into the significance of celebrating your manifestations and successes along your journey of harnessing the universe's energy for success. As we explore the mindful universe paradox and the six steps to manifesting your biggest life intention, it is important to acknowledge the power of celebrating milestones, big or small, as they contribute to your overall growth and well-being.

RECOGNIZING THE POWER OF CELEBRATION:

Celebration is not just an indulgence in joyful moments; it is a powerful tool that amplifies the energy of gratitude and attracts more abundance into your life. By celebrating your manifestations and successes, you reinforce positive affirmations and solidify your connection with the universe. This practice not only enhances your self-belief but also strengthens your manifestation abilities.

ACKNOWLEDGING THE SMALL WINS:
Often, we become so focused on achieving our ultimate goals that we overlook the small victories that pave the way. By acknowledging and celebrating these smaller wins, you imbue your journey with a sense of joy and fulfillment, motivating you to keep moving forward. Remember, success is not solely defined by grand achievements but also by the progress made along the way.

CREATING RITUALS OF CELEBRATION:
Developing rituals of celebration allows you to honor your manifestations and successes in a meaningful way. Whether it's lighting a candle, journaling your achievements, or sharing your triumphs with loved ones, these rituals help anchor your manifestations into reality and create a positive feedback loop with the universe. By incorporating celebration into your daily or weekly routine, you

cultivate a mindset of abundance and attract more opportunities for success.

Sharing Your Successes:

Celebrating your manifestations and successes is not just for your personal gratification. Sharing your achievements with others not only inspires and uplifts those around you but also strengthens your manifestation abilities. By acknowledging and sharing your successes, you become a beacon of positivity and attract even more abundance, creating a ripple effect of manifestation in the universe.

In the journey of manifesting your biggest life intention, celebrating your manifestations and successes is a crucial step. By recognizing the power of celebration, acknowledging the small wins, creating rituals, and sharing your successes, you not only cultivate a mindset of abundance but also strengthen your connection with the universe. Remember, every manifestation and success is a testament to your power and alignment with the universe's energy. So, embrace the power of celebration and let it fuel your journey towards success and fulfillment.

Embracing a Mindset of Gratitude and Abundance

In the journey towards success and fulfillment, one of the most powerful mindsets we can adopt is that of gratitude and abundance. This mindset, explored in this subchapter, is a key element of harnessing the universe's energy for success. Whether you are an entrepreneur, a student, a parent, or simply someone seeking personal growth, cultivating a mindset of gratitude and abundance can transform your life.

Gratitude is the practice of recognizing and appreciating the blessings and positive aspects of our lives. It involves acknowledging the abundance that already exists and shifting our focus from what we lack to what we have. When we are grateful, we tap into the infinite potential of the universe, opening ourselves up to opportunities and possibilities that align with our desires.

By embracing gratitude, we create a positive ripple effect that extends beyond ourselves. Our energy attracts more positive experiences, relationships, and resources into our lives. In fact, research has shown that practicing gratitude can improve our mental and physical well-being, enhance our relationships, and boost our overall happiness.

Abundance, on the other hand, is the belief that there is more than enough for everyone. It is the understanding that the universe is abundant and willing to provide us with what we need and desire. When we adopt an abundance mindset, we let go of scarcity and lack, allowing ourselves to receive and give freely.

To cultivate a mindset of gratitude and abundance, it is important to practice daily gratitude rituals. This can include keeping a gratitude journal, where we write down three things we are grateful for each day. Additionally, expressing gratitude to others, whether through thank-you notes or verbal appreciation, strengthens our sense of connection and creates a positive feedback loop.

Another powerful tool for embracing abundance is visualization. By vividly imagining our desired outcomes and embodying the emotions associated with their achievement, we align ourselves with the energy of abundance. This practice helps us manifest our biggest life intentions by attracting the people, circumstances, and opportunities that support our goals.

In conclusion, embracing a mindset of gratitude and abundance is a transformative practice that can unlock the universe's energy for success. By cultivating gratitude and recognizing the abundance that surrounds us, we open ourselves up to infinite possibilities and attract positive experiences into our lives. Whether you are seeking personal growth or professional success, adopting this mindset can propel you towards your biggest life intentions. Begin your journey of embracing gratitude and abundance today, and witness the magic unfold in your life.

Living a Purposeful and Intentional Life

In our fast-paced world filled with distractions and demands, it's easy to lose sight of our true purpose and live on autopilot. We find ourselves drifting through life, feeling unfulfilled and wondering why we aren't experiencing the success and happiness we crave. But what if there was a way to harness the universe's energy and manifest our biggest life intentions? Welcome to the subchapter "Living a Purposeful and Intentional Life" from the book "The Vacuum Effect: Harnessing the Universe's Energy for Success."

This subchapter is addressed to everyone, because regardless of age, background, or current circumstances, each one of us has the power to live a purposeful and intentional life. It is also specifically tailored for the niches of the "Mindful Universe Paradox: The Universe hates a vacuum: Six steps to manifest your biggest life intention." If you've ever felt stuck, lost, or unsure of your life's direction, this subchapter is for you.

Living a purposeful and intentional life begins with self-awareness. It's about understanding who you are, what truly matters to you, and what you want to achieve. By aligning your actions with your core values and passions, you can create a life that is meaningful and fulfilling. This subchapter will guide you through six transformative steps to manifest your biggest life intention:

1. DEFINE YOUR PURPOSE: UNCOVER YOUR UNIQUE purpose by reflecting on your passions, strengths, and values. What brings you joy? What makes you feel alive? By understanding your purpose, you can set clear intentions for your life.

2. SET MEANINGFUL GOALS: IDENTIFY SPECIFIC, measurable, achievable, relevant, and time-bound goals that align with your purpose. These goals will serve as guideposts on your journey towards living a purposeful life.

3. CULTIVATE MINDFULNESS: DEVELOP A MINDFUL approach to life, being fully present in each moment. By practicing mindfulness, you can deepen your self-awareness, enhance your focus, and make conscious choices that align with your purpose.

4. TAKE INSPIRED ACTION: MOVE BEYOND INTENTION and take inspired action towards your goals. Break them down into manageable steps and commit to consistent progress. The universe responds to intentional action, and by taking steps towards your dreams, you create momentum.

5. EMBRACE RESILIENCE: CHALLENGES AND SETBACKS are inevitable, but they don't define you. Embrace resilience and view obstacles as opportunities for growth. Learn from failures, adapt your approach, and never lose sight of your purpose.

6. Practice Gratitude: Cultivate a grateful mindset and celebrate each step forward. Gratitude opens doors to abundance and attracts positive energy. By acknowledging and appreciating what you have, you create space for more blessings to flow into your life.

Living a purposeful and intentional life is a journey, and this subchapter will equip you with the tools and mindset needed to navigate it successfully. Remember, you have the power to manifest your biggest life intentions. Embrace the vacuum effect and harness the universe's energy to create a life that is aligned with your true purpose. Start living intentionally today and watch as the universe conspires to support your journey towards success and fulfillment.

Twenty-five personal stories utilizing the vacuum effect:

1. The Desert Whisperer. As Sarah drove through the vast desert, she realized that the vacuum of solitude allowed her mind to focus on her intentions. She set her goal to find inner peace amidst the barren landscape, and with each passing mile, her mind became a calm oasis.

2. The Coastal Meditation. Along the coastal highway, Mark opened his car windows to the soothing

sound of crashing waves. He harnessed the vacuum effect to set a mindful intention of letting go of stress and anxiety. With the ocean breeze in his hair, he felt his worries wash away.

3. MOUNTAIN MANIFESTATION. AS JENNIFER ASCENDED the winding mountain road, she visualized her dreams coming true. The isolation of the mountains helped her concentrate on her intentions, and with each curve, she became more confident in her path.

4. SUNSET SERENITY. DRIVING WEST INTO A mesmerizing sunset, Alex made a conscious effort to appreciate life's beauty. With the sun sinking below the horizon, he set an intention to cherish every moment, basking in the vacuum of serenity.

5. HIGHWAY OF GRATITUDE. EMILY EMBARKED ON A cross-country road trip, using the open road to cultivate gratitude. She focused on her intention of appreciating the small things in life, making each mile a reminder of the blessings she possessed.

6. RAINY DAY REFLECTIONS. ON A RAINY DAY, DANIEL found himself stuck in traffic. Instead of frustration, he embraced the vacuum effect to reflect on his life. He decided to be more patient and understanding, starting with the traffic jam.

7. FOREST RETREAT. AS LILY DROVE THROUGH THE dense forest, the towering trees made her feel small yet connected. She harnessed the vacuum effect to set an intention of becoming more grounded and in tune with nature.

8. CITYSCAPE MINDFULNESS. IN THE HEART OF THE bustling city, Carlos sat in his parked car, meditating on the cacophony of sounds around him. Through the urban chaos, he aimed to find inner peace, using the vacuum effect to drown out distractions.

9. FAMILY BONDING. THE FAMILY SET OUT ON A ROAD trip, using the journey to strengthen their connections. They vowed to put away their devices and engage with one another, making the most of the time spent together.

10. HEALING DRIVE. AFTER A TOUGH BREAKUP, MAYA hit the road with a heavy heart. She used the vacuum effect

to process her emotions and set an intention to heal and grow from the experience.

11. STARLIT DREAMS. UNDER A BLANKET OF STARS, Tom parked his car in a remote area. He gazed at the night sky, setting an intention to reach for his dreams. Each star became a reminder of his aspirations.

12. ROADSIDE RECONCILIATION. SARAH AND DAVID, long-time friends, embarked on a road trip to mend their strained relationship. In the confined space of the car, they resolved to communicate openly and rebuild their bond.

13. HISTORICAL REFLECTION. EMMA DROVE THROUGH A historic town, allowing herself to be transported to another era. She set an intention to learn from the past and carry forward the wisdom of those who came before her.

14. ARTISTIC INSPIRATION. CLARA, AN ARTIST, traveled through picturesque landscapes. She aimed to harness the vacuum effect to find inspiration for her next masterpiece, absorbing the natural beauty around her.

15. RANDOM ACTS OF KINDNESS. ON A BUSY FREEWAY, Mark decided to use the vacuum effect to cultivate kindness. He made a pact to perform one random act of kindness for a stranger at each pit stop, leaving positivity in his wake.

16. RURAL REJUVENATION. EXHAUSTED BY CITY LIFE, James sought solace in rural areas. The quiet countryside allowed him to set an intention of rejuvenation and self-care, finding peace in simplicity.

17. BRIDGING DIFFERENCES. TWO POLITICAL ACTIVISTS from opposing parties embarked on a road trip together. In the car's confined space, they aimed to use the vacuum effect to find common ground and build bridges.

18. WANDERING SOUL. SARAH EMBRACED A NOMADIC lifestyle, living on the road. She set an intention to discover her true self through travel, finding purpose in the journey rather than the destination.

19. ROADSIDE ENLIGHTENMENT. THOMAS PARKED HIS car at a scenic overlook and meditated. He aimed to harness the vacuum effect to gain clarity about his life's purpose and find the path that truly resonated with him.

20. HIGHWAY HEALING. AFTER A PERSONAL LOSS, Jessica used long drives to heal her grief. The open road allowed her to set an intention of accepting her feelings and finding hope amid sorrow.

21. RIVER OF FORGIVENESS. DRIVING ALONGSIDE A winding river, Mia contemplated her past mistakes. She harnessed the vacuum effect to forgive herself and others, allowing the flow of the river to symbolize the release of burdens.

22. TRAFFIC PATIENCE. STUCK IN A NEVER-ENDING traffic jam, John set an intention to practice patience and mindfulness. He realized that even amidst chaos, he could find tranquility within himself and embrace the silence.

23. CROSSING BOUNDARIES. AS RACHEL CROSSED STATE lines, she reflected on the significance of boundaries in life. She aimed to use the vacuum effect to break free from self-imposed limitations and explore new horizons. She decided to create some new personal boundaries to explore her belief set.

24. ROADSIDE RESOLUTIONS. ON NEW YEAR'S DAY, A group of friends drove to a remote location. They set intentions for the year ahead, vowing to support one another in achieving their goals.

25. JOYFUL JOURNEY. TIM AND LISA CELEBRATED THEIR love by embarking on a road trip together. They aimed to use the vacuum effect to infuse joy into their relationship, making every mile an adventure of happiness.

Conclusion: Embracing the Vacuum Effect for Lasting Transformation

Regenerate Cha

In this journey through "The Vacuum Effect: Harnessing the Universe's Energy for Success," we have explored the profound power of the universe and its ability to shape our lives. From understanding the Mindful Universe Paradox to manifesting our biggest life intentions, we have delved into the remarkable potential that lies within each of us.

The notion that the universe hates a vacuum may seem counterintuitive at first, but as we have discovered, it holds a powerful truth. Just as nature abhors a physical vacuum, the universe abhors an energetic one. It constantly seeks to fill any voids, whether they are physical, mental, or emotional. By embracing this understanding, we can tap into the transformative energy that surrounds us and create lasting change in our lives.

The six steps to manifesting our biggest life intentions have provided a roadmap for harnessing the vacuum effect. We began by setting clear and specific intentions, aligning our thoughts and emotions with our desires. This step alone can have a profound impact on our lives, as it allows us to focus our energy and direct it towards our goals.

Next, we explored the power of visualization and the role it plays in manifesting our intentions. By vividly imagining the outcome we desire, we activate the law of attraction and draw it closer to us. Coupled with regular meditation and mindfulness practices, this step helps us to remain present and open to the opportunities that arise.

Taking inspired action was another crucial step in our journey. We learned that the universe responds to our efforts and rewards our commitment. By taking consistent and purposeful action towards our goals, we create a momentum that propels us forward.

Throughout this book, we have emphasized the importance of gratitude and trust in the process. By expressing gratitude for what we have and trusting that the universe will provide, we cultivate a positive mindset that attracts abundance and opportunities.

In conclusion, the vacuum effect is a powerful tool that can transform our lives if we embrace it. By understanding and harnessing the energy of the universe, we can manifest our biggest life intentions and create a reality that aligns with our desires. The key lies in remaining mindful, focused, and open to the possibilities that surround us. Let us embark on this journey together, embracing the vacuum effect and experiencing the lasting transformation it can bring to our lives.

In the realm of self-help and personal development, it is crucial to understand that each individual's journey is unique. The book " " aims to guide readers from all walks of life on a path towards manifesting their biggest life intentions. However, it is important to note that the chapter and sub-chapter titles provided in this book are general and may require further refinement based on the specific content and focus of the book.

The author recognizes that everyone's desires and goals are different. While the book addresses a broad audience, it also caters to niche interests, one of which is the "Mindful Universe Paradox: The Universe hates a vacuum: Six steps to manifest your biggest life intention." This subchapter delves into the concept of the universe's energy and how it influences our ability to manifest our desires.

The author acknowledges that specific information may be lacking, and, therefore, encourages readers to further explore and refine the chapter and sub-chapter titles based on their unique circumstances. By doing so, readers can align the book's guidance with their specific goals, making the content more relatable and actionable.

Understanding the mindful universe paradox is a key aspect of harnessing the universe's energy for success. The subchapter offers six practical steps that readers can take to manifest their biggest life intentions. These steps serve as a guide to help individuals tap into the universe's energy and leverage it to bring their desires into reality.

By acknowledging the need for further refinement in the chapter and sub-chapter titles, the author demonstrates a commitment to providing readers with tailored guidance. This empowers individuals to personalize their reading experience and apply the teachings in a way that resonates with their unique circumstances.

"The Vacuum Effect: Harnessing the Universe's Energy for Success" is a book that recognizes the individuality of its audience and aims to provide relevant insights and strategies to help them manifest their biggest life intentions.

Through mindful exploration and refinement, readers can unlock the full potential of the universe's energy and embrace a path towards success and fulfillment.

Manifest your biggest desire!

Acknowledgments

Thanks to all my beautiful friends and family who supported me and made this book possible.